ULTIMATE THRILL SPORTS

WHITEWATER SPORTS

By Deb Pinniger

Gareth Stevens
Publishing

Please visit our web site at www.garethstevens.com
For a free catalog describing our list of high-quality books, call 1-800-542-2595 (USA) or
1-800-387-3178 (Canada). Our fax: 1-877-542-2596

Library of Congress Cataloging-in-Publication Data available upon request from publisher.

ISBN-10: 0-8368-8965-7   ISBN-13: 978-0-8368-8965-9 (lib. binding)

This U.S. edition copyright © 2008 by Gareth Stevens, Inc. Original edition copyright © 2007 by ticktock Media Ltd, First published in Great Britain in 2007 by ticktock Media Ltd., Unit 2, Orchard Business Centre, North Farm Road, Tunbridge Wells, Kent, TN2 3XF

ticktock project editor: Julia Adams
ticktock project designer: Sara Greasley
ticktock picture researcher: Lizzie Knowles
editor: Ben Hubbard

Gareth Stevens Senior Managing Editor: Lisa M. Guidone
Gareth Stevens Creative Director: Lisa Donovan
Gareth Stevens Graphic Designer: Giovanni Cipolla
Gareth Stevens Associate Editor: Amanda Hudson

Picture credits (t=top; b=bottom; c=center; l=left; r=right): AFP/Getty Images: 36. Manual Arnu: 22t, 29t, 57b. Bryan & Cherry Alexander Photography/Alamy: 9t. Darren Baker: 32/33t, 54/55t, 54b, 55b. BristolK/Alamy: 35t. Nico Chassing: 15c. Mike Hamel: 17b, 42, 46, 50b. Tommy Hilleke: 61. Tanya Faux: 56b. Erik Jackson: 59cl, 59tr. Kristine Jackson: 56t. Japan Rafters Federation: 30, 31t, 31b. Johnnie Kern: 25c. Jens Klatt: 32b. Cameron Lawson: 33b. John MacGregor, A Thousand Miles in the Rob Roy Canoe: 9b. Charlie Munsey/Corbis: 25t. Desre Pickers: 26/27t, 26b, 27bl, 27br. Deb Pinniger: 4/5, 6/7t, 6b, 10/11, 13t, 13cl, 14 all, 15t, 16b, 17t, 18/19, 20, 21t, 21b, 23t, 28t, 29c, 35b, 37t, 37b, 40/41, 43 all, 44, 45 all, 47t, 48/49, 50/51t, 58t. Aaryn Powell: 52. Robert Preston/Alamy: 24. Geraint Rowlands: 47b. Shutterstock: 1, 2, 3, 7b, 8, 12t, 14/15 background, 53t. Jason Smith: 23c. 38, 39t, 39b. Ticktock Media Archive: 60. Tom Uhlman/Alamy: 51c. Paul Williams/Action Plus: 16t. Jeff Wolfram/Alamy: 34.

Every effort has been made to trace the copyright holders for the photos used in this book, and the publisher apologizes in advance for any unintentional omissions. We would be pleased to insert the appropriate acknowledgements in any subsequent edition of this publication.

Printed in the United States of America

1 2 3 4 5 6 7 8 9 10 09 08

Contents

chapter 1: whitewater

Steve Fisher, one of the greatest whitewater paddlers ever, heads toward a massive hole on the Zambezi River's famous rapid number nine in Zambia, Africa.

Whitewater rafting and kayaking are practiced all over the world, from New Zealand and China to Iceland and Iran. Whitewater sports let individuals explore the unique, and often secret, world of rivers.

Paddlers explore whitewater in all sorts of ways. Some surf big waves doing aerial tricks. Others enjoy expeditions, such as spending ten days in the Himalayas carrying their equipment in their kayaks. Paddlers even run some of the world's largest tourist-attraction waterfalls.

Whitewater kayaking is a sport that attracts all types of people – men and women, young and old alike.

Wherever there are rivers, there are paddlers searching for the ultimate whitewater experience.

The opportunities are endless. But any whitewater sport can be dangerous. Proper instruction and guidance are a must. Luckily, many kayak schools offer superb courses.

The key ingredients for whitewater sports are water and air. When water moves quickly over rocks in a steep river, air gets trapped in the water, causing it to look white. This sets the stage for fun!

Water is an incredibly strong element. Any whitewater paddler needs plenty of training to master it.

Today, people paddle for pleasure. But thousands of years ago, these skills were crucial to survival. North and South American Indians, along with the Polynesian islanders of the Pacific, used canoes for hunting, fishing, and travel.

Early Canoes

Ancient rafts and canoes were made from a variety of natural materials, such as reed. In fact, reed canoes are still used today on the Nile River in Egypt and on Lake Titicaca, bordering Bolivia and Peru. The oldest known canoe was found in the tomb of a Sumerian king near the Euphrates River (in modern-day Iraq). This raft is estimated to be about 6,000 years old.
Although canoes are still in use today, they are not very popular for whitewater sports.

A traditional reed raft floats on Lake Titicaca.

For Survival

Inuits of the Arctic developed what is called a closed-cockpit kayak. Covering, or closing, the top of the kayak kept the icy waters of the Arctic Ocean from filling the kayak. The Inuits' kayaks had whalebone and driftwood frames, with sea lion skin stretched tightly over them. The whole thing was waterproofed with whale fat. Inuits' kayaks were their lifeline, allowing them to hunt and fish every day.

For Sport

It was John MacGregor, a British lawyer, who made canoeing popular as a sport in Europe and the United States in the late 19th century. He designed a boat similar to the closed-cockpit kayaks used by the Inuits.

John MacGregor canoes through Tuttlingen, Germany.

chapter 2: the water

Many paddlers set out on long treks just to find the perfect whitewater. This group is exploring the canyon on the Upper Mendoza River in Argentina.

It is vital for any paddler to know how tough a stretch of water is going to be. There are six grades, or classes, used to describe water. The easiest is Grade 1. The highest, Grade 6, is so difficult that only the most experienced paddlers can survive it.

The international scale of river difficulty grades water on both the technical difficulty and the danger associated with a stretch of river or a single rapid. It also gives the paddler an idea what skill level is required to undertake this particular section of water.

Picking a route through the
Isonzo River in Slovenia

Kayaker Erik Martinsonn descends into the
white foam of the Ulvua River in Norway.

Because water changes, grades change
too. For example, there can be a hard
Grade 2, easy Grade 3, or hard Grade
5. The grade of a river or a rapid can
change as the water level changes, such
as after heavy rain or when mountain
snow melts in spring.

More water usually makes
rapids more powerful and
difficult, although they can
become easier if the water
covers hazards such as
boulders. When a river is in
flood stage, or "spate," the
fast-flowing water may
create lots of pressure and
become very dangerous.
Flooded rivers are also
extremely hazardous to
navigate. They should
only be undertaken by
expert paddlers. If a
kayaker exits the kayak
in a flooded river,
rescuing the kayaker and
his or her equipment can
be dangerous.

Exit a kayak Fall out of the
kayak into the water.

For paddlers, matching their skills to the water's grade means understanding terms such as "boil," "whirlpool," "ledge," and "drop." Paddlers also need to know if they're up to the grade before getting on the water.

Grade 1

This is easy whitewater. It has a regular current, small waves, and simple obstacles to navigate.

Grade 2

This grade has fairly difficult whitewater, with clear, open passages. The current can change, with medium-sized waves, holes, and obstacles to navigate around.

Grade 3

This is difficult whitewater! The passage is clear but has high waves, holes, and boils, not to mention boulders and other obstacles.

Grade 4

If a paddler is in a rapid at this grade, he or she needs to get out of the boat to find a clear line. The water pressure is strong, with big waves, strong holes, boils, whirlpools, boulders, ledges, and drops.

Grade 5

This whitewater is extremely difficult. Each rapid needs careful thought, as often the only safe route is very narrow. High waves with strong holes and pressure areas are some of the challenges that the paddler will meet.

Grade 6

By now, the paddler is at the limit! Grade 6 is usually only possible to navigate at certain water levels. Even then, it is extremely dangerous and can be life-threatening. Grade 6 is for experienced professionals only.

Boil A place in the water where two currents meet. The pressure of both currents is very strong, which makes for a powerful collision and masses of whitewater.

Boulder A large rock

Drop Any spot where flowing water drops suddenly, possibly creating a waterfall

Hole A feature in the river where turbulent water returns on itself, creating pressure or suction. Some holes can be life-threatening.

Ledge The upper lip or edge of a drop

Rapid A section of a river where the riverbed is relatively steep, which increases the speed and turbulence of the water flow

Whirlpool A swirling body of water under the surface

Pool Drop

Pool drop rivers have equal measures of rapids and calmer water. After each rapid, the water pools out at the bottom, making it great for people learning to paddle. Many of these rivers are found in California and Norway.

Alpine

These rivers aren't for beginners, but they are lots of fun for experienced paddlers. They drop very quickly in height, so they are very steep and have fast-flowing water, making it hard to stop at times.

Volume The amount of water in the river

High-volume

Although they may not be very steep, these wide rivers gather their water from a large area. This means that they end up with big, bouncy rapids and good surfing waves. They also tend to have fewer obstacles and make for a really fun ride! The Nile and Zambezi rivers in Africa have become a home for freestyle kayakers wanting to perfect their acrobatic tricks on big waves.

Steep Creeks

These slim rivers are extremely steep, lower-volume, and narrow, with lots of little drops, waterfalls, and slides. The riverbed is often bedrock. There are many fun steep creeks in the northern part of the Italian Alps, as well as in California.

chapter 3:

whitewater sports

British freestyling pro Matt Cooke enjoys some paddling on the impressive Falls of Lora, Scotland.

Whitewater river running is all about sharing exciting adventures that test paddlers' skills as they make their way safely to the bottom of a river. For some, it could be paddling a Grade 1 river, while others live for the buzz of a Grade 5 creek!

A pair of paddlers explore the San Giovanni River, Italy.

Whitewater kayaking in a remote part of the world, with a small group of friends, gives paddlers an amazing sense of freedom.

Running a whitewater river safely requires teamwork, strategy, and careful planning. Paddlers usually go out in groups of at least three people so they can work as a team, keeping each other safe. Together, the paddlers break down their route into a series of individual challenges that can be tackled safely by working as a unit. Clear communication is vital. The roaring water means that hand signals are the only sure way of getting a message across.

River running has advanced tremendously since the early days of the sport. Strong plastic kayaks give paddlers lots of control and keep them safe. Paddlers now use a dynamic and athletic style of paddling, as well as better techniques than in the "old days," so they have more control than ever. This is pushing river running to new heights.

Sophisticated kayaks allow pros like Britain's Andy Phillips to master even the trickiest of passages.

The huge and overwhelming water masses of the Indus River in Pakistan

Expedition kayaking has been called the ultimate whitewater adventure. Negotiating the course of an unknown river takes skill, knowledge, and planning. Only the most determined kayakers can pull it off.

Whitewater expeditions usually take place in remote areas of the world. The rivers are set in dense jungles, hidden canyons, or high mountain ranges. Often the only way to reach these remote rivers is by kayak, which makes expedition kayaking unique. An expedition demands real commitment. It can take days to follow the river through challenging terrain. Usually only a small, dedicated team of up to four people can complete such an undertaking.

The Bachrati River in Iran's Zagros Mountains is one of the world's most impressive canyons.

Expedition kayakers take a range of equipment with them, such as the following:

- video and camera equipment
- sleeping bags and mats
- tents
- cooking pans and stoves
- all their food
- satellite phone and maps
- spare paddles
- rescue equipment
- clothes

Camping out on the banks of the Kanali River in Nepal

Paddlers use normal whitewater kayaks but cleverly store their supplies and equipment in the spaces under and behind their seats, as well as in the front by their footrests. Waterproof bags are used to keep everything dry.

Adventurous kayakers have undertaken some incredible whitewater expeditions over the years. In modern times, these range from the heroic descent of the Blue Nile River to what is probably the greatest kayak expedition of our time — the Tsangpo Expedition.

Blue Nile waterfalls near Bahir Dar, Ethiopia (Africa)

Blue Nile River

In 1972, Mike Jones and Mick Hopkinson from Britain led the alpine descent of the Blue Nile River in Ethiopia. They ran a longer section of the river, with much bigger rapids, than had ever been done before. During the expedition, they encountered Nile crocodiles, ferocious hippos, and dangerous rapids.

Tsangpo Expedition

In 2002, American expedition paddler Scott Lindgren led 96 team members on the first descent of the Tsangpo Gorge in Tibet. It took place during the freezing Himalayan winter, when the river's waters were at their lowest level. At its core, the team had seven international paddlers with a wealth of experience in river exploration.

Scott Lindgren scouts a section of rapids on the Tsangpo River.

The team at Tsangpo River in Tibet in 2002. The paddlers, from left to right: Johnnie Kern, Allan Ellard, Mike Abbott, Willie Kern, Scott Lindgren, Dustin Knapp, and Steve

The mighty Tsangpo Gorge is the deepest river gorge in the world. Simply by entering the gorge, Scott and his team made kayaking history. Their expedition was a complete success. By exploring farther into the gorge than anyone else before them, the team raised the bar in expedition paddling.

Alpine descent A steep river with fast-flowing water

On April 10, 2007, South African kayaker Hendri Cortez set out to paddle the Murchison Falls section of the White Nile River in Uganda – one of the most dangerous sections of any river in the world. His goal was to complete this notorious 50-mile (80-kilometer) stretch on his own! Hendri Cortez knew what he was taking on. The Murchison Falls section of the White Nile – famous for its extreme whitewater – had been successfully kayaked only four times. Three of those trips were by Hendri and his team. So he knew, more than anyone else, the dangers he would face going solo. He would be exposed to dangerous rapids and wildlife.

Hendri had to make absolutely sure his equipment was intact. His life depended on it.

The view from just below the Murchison Falls

Murchison Falls is famous not just for its whitewater but also for the wild animals found there. There are more hippos in this stretch of river than anywhere else in the world. Hippos are known to aggressively defend their territory. They can be even more dangerous than crocodiles! Hendri paddled fast, concentrating on every piece of water. He dodged all the dangers and completed this amazing feat in just two days.

Hendri had to move carefully to avoid the aggressive native hippos.

Hendri had to prove himself in many Grade 5 rapids, like this one.

Whitewater rafting is the perfect activity for anyone with a sense of adventure who is looking for an exciting physical challenge. Led by experienced guides, groups in inflatable rubber rafts ride hair-raising rapids on some of our planet's greatest rivers.

Rafting is probably the oldest method of river transportation in the world. For thousands of years, people have used rafts to carry food and essential supplies. As a recreational sport, whitewater rafting grew in popularity during the late 1970s. Today, it is more popular than ever. Rafting companies in countries from Indonesia to Iceland now offer expeditions.

Preparing for a big drop on the Zambezi River in Zambia

A view of the impressive Karakoram Mountains from the Indus River in Pakistan

Rafting provides an incredible experience for a team of people.

Rafting trips offer amazing experiences. Imagine traveling down the mighty Zambezi River in Africa for seven days. The only people to be seen on the journey are local villagers collecting water and fishermen catching their dinner from the river.

American river explorer Richard Bangs led pioneering expeditions during the late 1970s and 1980s that opened up some of the world's greatest rivers.

Here are just a few places that now offer whitewater rafting experiences — all thanks to Richard's sense of adventure!

- Indus River, Pakistan
- Omo River, Ethiopia
- Yangtze River, China

Brazil versus Japan in the 2007 World Rafting Championships sprint

t was not until the 1990s that rafting became included in major game events. Since then, however, it has grown quickly in popularity. Countries from around the world began competing in various disciplines, and in 1998 these events became world championships. Rafting competitions consist of three disciplines: sprint, slalom, and downriver. The points from each are added together to determine the overall winner. Each team has six members, with the option to have a reserve.

Sprint

The sprint is the most visually exciting discipline and counts for 30 percent of the points. It is an elimination race in which pairs of teams race down a section of powerful rapids.

Elimination race A race that consists of heats of pairs racing down rapids. The winner of each heat proceeds to the next round, with two teams remaining for the final.

Brazil competes in the 2003 slalom event.

Slalom

The slalom is the most technically challenging discipline and counts for 30 percent of the points. High levels of technique and teamwork are needed to negotiate through twelve downriver and upriver gates in rapids. Touching, failing to pass, or intentionally moving a gate results in a penalty.

Israel and South Africa in the 2001 downriver event on the Zambezi River

Downriver

The downriver event is worth 40 percent of the points. The event is close to an hour of racing along a section of continuous and powerful rapids. Technical ability and endurance are essential elements to ensure a good position in this event. The points earned by the teams in the previous events determine their position in the starting lineup in groups of up to five rafts.

A revolution in boat design made the sport of creek boating possible. Until the mid-1980s, paddlers used long, fragile fiberglass boats. The Topolino kayak changed all that — and the sport has never looked back.

Creek boating is the most extreme form of kayaking. It involves paddling down very steep waterfalls and low water-volume creeks. Long boats were extremely difficult to maneuver on these steep, rocky rivers. The small, specially designed Topolino is just 7.2 feet (2.2 meters) long, making it ideal for creeking. Creek boats need to be short and maneuverable so they are buoyant and sit well on the water surface.

Ripping waterfalls, such as this one in Norway, can only be mastered in an extremely maneuverable kayak.

WHITEWATER

British pro kayaker Shaun Baker masters the Rauma River in Norway in his Topolino.

Boats with rounded ends, like the Topolino, are also less likely to get stuck on underwater rocks when paddlers jump off waterfalls and drops.

Many paddlers learn how to cope with the impact of landing after a big drop from sports like skiing and mountain biking. Paddlers found they needed to make their bodies absorb the shock — like a spring. By positioning themselves forward as they land, they can absorb most of the impact energy through their bodies. If they don't do this, they risk breaking bones or suffering other serious injuries.

Extreme kayaking races include many big drops, like this one on Upper Cherry Creek in California.

Freestyle kayaking is the youngest whitewater sport. Playboating, as it is often called, is a gymnastic form of kayaking. Paddlers perform tricks that require the highest levels of precision, technique, balance, coordination, and spatial awareness.

Static Water

Freestyle kayakers perform their tricks on a static piece of water, like a hole. This means that the shape and size of the hole stay the same. The kayakers use small, agile kayaks with a concentrated volume that can be popped into the air easily. Most freestyle kayaking is done on just a small stretch of water, allowing paddlers repeated opportunities to improve their skills.

Concentrated volume The volume of a kayak that gives it maximum buoyancy

Play Runs

Most rivers used for freestyle have small sections known to local paddlers as "play runs." They consist of various waves and holes where paddlers can practice their latest moves.

Championships

Every two years, freestylers compete at the World Freestyle Championships at varying locations around the world. There are 98 competitors (both male and female) and 36 junior competitors (under 18). Each paddler has 45 seconds to perform his or her chosen moves and gets the highest scores for difficulty of moves, combinations, and managing to jump completely out of the water.

Whitewater slalom racing isn't just a battle with the river; it's also a race against the clock. The competitors negotiate a series of gates on the river, each of which they must pass through. It is one of the few whitewater disciplines in which competing teams use canoes.

Slalom gates are two poles hung from wires over the river. They are colored either green (downstream) or red (upstream), indicating the direction they must be negotiated in. Upstream gates mean the paddler has to go against the current to pass the gate and then proceed downstream again. Most slalom courses take 80 to 120 seconds for the fastest paddlers to complete. Paddlers compete in teams or solo. Time penalties are given if paddlers miss gates or touch them. Precision is the key to successfully competing in whitewater slalom.

Paddling together as a two-person team, or crew, is hard work. Each paddler needs to know exactly what the other is doing to keep the boat on course. The paddler at the back steers the boat. The front paddler is mostly responsible for the boat's speed.

A French crew goes for gold on the finish line at the 2006 European Slalom Championships in France.

Scottish Olympic silver medalist Campbell Walsh competes at the 2006 European Slalom Championships in France.

Whitewater slalom racing is an Olympic sport. Competitors at the Olympic slalom races use sleek, carbon fiber kayaks that are 11.5 feet (6.7 m) long and weigh 22 pounds (10 kilograms). Paddlers race down more than 984 feet (300 m) of whitewater through 20 to 25 gates. Olympic runs take fast paddlers about 140 seconds to complete. Other international slalom competitions include the European and World Championships and the World Cup. European paddlers dominate the sport at the international level. This isn't surprising, given that kayaking is the national sport of Slovakia and is hugely popular throughout Europe.

Squirt boating evolved when slalom racers started to dip the stern (or back) of the boat under the water's surface. This new maneuver was named a tail squirt. Paddlers developed this new technique to the point where they were able to get their boats vertical.

A squirt boater performs a Cartwheel.

Squirt boaters use both the river's surface and underwater currents. Paddlers perform tricks like Cartwheels, where the boat is rotated vertically from end to end. In one trick, the Mystery Move, the paddler disappears completely underwater yet still travels along in full control. Paddlers use these squirt boating tricks to expand their skills in whitewater and improve their control over their boat.

Squirt boats can be custom-made to a paddler's weight and size so they fit like a glove.

Squirt boats were developed from slalom boats. It started when American paddler Jessie Whitmore cut down several old slalom boats, making them much smaller and easier to maneuver. Eventually, U.S. kayak designer and freestyle paddler Jim Snyder made the first amazing short boat. Squirt boating was born!

Squirt boats are generally half the volume of normal kayaks. Although they are designed to float, they sit so low in the water that most of the boat and the paddler appear to be under the water's surface.

chapter 4: the gear

Paddling through heavy whitewater currents requires the right equipment in order to be as protected as possible. Paddlers need to stay dry, warm, afloat, and visible at all times.

Helmet

Life jacket

Spray skirt deck

Spray skirt tunnel

Paddlers not only brave the harsh water but are also exposed to extreme weather. Their equipment is designed to protect them against these conditions and provide maximum safety.

A kayaker in full gear. With the exception of the spray skirt, paddlers use exactly the same gear as rafters.

42

Helmet

A helmet is essential for all whitewater paddlers, as head injuries from boulders and rocks in the water can be extremely dangerous. The helmet must provide all-around protection and fit snugly.

Life Jacket

Sometimes called a PFD (personal flotation device), a life jacket allows paddlers to float safely in the water if they exit their kayaks. The jacket also has padding (to protect them from sharp rocks) and adjustable straps (for a perfect fit).

Spray Skirt

The spray skirt covers a kayak's cockpit to keep out the water. The paddler wears the tunnel part around the waist, while a tight elastic bungee cord snaps the deck around the cockpit's rim. Spray skirts need to be strong enough to withstand the pressure of the river.

Safety Equipment

A 50- to 65-foot (15- to 20-m) length of throw rope that floats is essential for each paddler. Most groups also carry a first-aid kit and a cell phone.

Waterproof and thermal clothing offers protection against a river's icy waters. Out of the water, raft and kayak paddlers wear strong, supportive shoes so they can move quickly over rough terrain without injuring their ankles.

Shoes

Shoes protect a paddler's feet from sharp rocks and cold water. They must provide support and give a good grip on rocks that are wet and slippery.

Dry Jacket

Jackets made from a breathable, waterproof fabric with latex neck and wrist seals and a double waist seal help keep paddlers dry.

Paddling Pants

Paddling pants are also made from a breathable, waterproof fabric. Latex or neoprene ankle and waist seals keep the paddler from getting wet.

Thermals

Paddlers wear thermal layers and fleeces under their waterproof jackets and pants to keep them warm.

Paddles and boats are essential pieces of whitewater equipment. Taking proper care of them can mean the difference between life and death.

Paddles

Paddles provide power and support in rapids. Breaking or dropping a paddle in difficult whitewater can be fatal to even the most skilled and experienced paddler. Many paddles are made from both fiberglass and carbon fiber. These materials make them very stiff and light. The strength of the blades gives the paddler a lot of power. Fiberglass shafts are flexible and can absorb the impact shock from hitting rocks.

Carbon fiber Very strong, lightweight material

46

back

seat

front

Kayaks

Whitewater kayaks are made of strong plastic. Vertical foam pillars in the front and back of the boat are an important safety feature. They give the boat strength and help maintain its shape. All whitewater boats have front and back handles to make them easy to carry.

Rafts

Rafts are made of very durable, multilayered rubber or vinyl fabrics. They are inflated with air, which keeps them afloat. In order to avoid punctures that might deflate the entire raft, the air is held in many separate chambers. Rafts also have inflated "crossbars" that stabilize the raft's shape. The length of a raft varies between 11 and 20 feet (3 and 6 m) and fits four to twelve people.

chapter 5:

people and places

Pro Tyler Curtis
enjoys the spectacular
limestone walls of the Grand
Canyon of the Verdon River in France.

Wherever there is whitewater, there is the opportunity for fun and adventure – it really is that simple! Knowing where to start looking for the best runs must be at the top of every paddler's agenda.

Africa

With many big-volume rivers, Africa offers some of the world's best whitewater experiences. The Zambezi and Nile rivers have become a popular place for kayakers. The Zambezi River is home to one of the latest paddling movements, called freeride. In the mid-1990s, some of the world's top kayakers lived and worked on the river day in and day out. This group pushed the sport to new heights. They performed tricks and running lines in big rapids that no one had previously thought possible.

Norway

Norway is one of the best and most beautiful places in the world for whitewater paddling. With a huge variety of amazing rivers to choose from, Norway has something for everyone.

United States

Every year, starting in the first week of September, the water volume of the Gauley River in West Virginia is increased to create ideal conditions for paddlers. "Controlled releases," which add huge amounts of water to the river in twenty-two stages over six weeks, transform this river into a world-class 9-mile (15-km) stretch of Grade 4 and 5 whitewater. This time of year is known as the Gauley Season.

Freeride Freestyle mixed with downriver paddling

Shaun Baker is an extreme kayaker. He is always pushing the boundaries to try something more daring than anyone else!

By the time he was 16 years old, the British paddler had kayaked some 700 miles (1,100 km) around mainland Britain. Since then he has excelled in freestyle and whitewater kayaking, holding the title of U.K. Freestyle Champion for nine years before discovering his passion for kayaking big waterfalls. His new quest is to find the biggest and best falls — and then to throw himself down them in his kayak!

Shaun has achieved the first descent of more than twenty major waterfalls, including some of the largest falls in Iceland and the Alps of up to 100 feet (160 km). His passion for finding new kayak challenges has led him to achieve more records than any other kayaker.

Shaun Baker on the 40-foot- (12-m-) high Godafoss Waterfall in Iceland, 2003

Not content to just kayak on water, Shaun became a pioneer of the land-speed record for a kayak. By using his kayak as a sled on the snow-covered peaks of the Canadian Rockies, he reached a top speed of 39.1 miles (62.9 km) per hour.

Shaun's most recent focus includes developing a jet-powered kayak. Some say these developments are not really kayaking, but Shaun has certainly pushed the boundaries of this extreme sport.

Shaun in his jet-powered kayak

Eric Jackson

This American's ability to succeed at any form of paddling has made him one of the best kayakers in the world and an Olympic champion. Slalom, extreme racing, and freestyle — he masters them all! Eric was ranked number one in the world in 2006 and has been freestyle champion four times.

Tanya Faux

Nicknamed the T-Bird, Australian world-class champion Tanya Faux is probably the best female freestyle paddler in the world. She was the first woman to undertake complex combo moves and remains one of the few to successfully execute them. Tanya has held the titles of Women's Big Air Freestyle Champion, Australian Whitewater Freestyle Kayak Champion, and 2004 International Freestyle Champion.

Combo moves Linked aerial moves

Niki Kelly

Niki is the most accomplished female whitewater kayaker ever. Whitewater, freestyle, expeditions — Niki's done it all and set new standards along the way. In 2004, this New Zealander completed the Seven Rivers Expedition in California, one of kayaking's biggest adventures. Niki ran California's seven top multi-day trips back to back. She paddled difficult Grade 5 rivers for fifty days in a row. These rivers included Kings River, San Joaquin, Kern River, Upper Cherry Creek on Tuolumne River, and Dinky Creek.

Olaf Obsommer

As one of the world's most accomplished expedition kayakers, Germany's Olaf Obsommer has been all over the world exploring the rivers of Canada, Montenegro, Malawi, Norway, Pakistan, and Réunion (in the Indian Ocean, east of Madagascar). He is one of the most important whitewater video artists and has directed some of the most influential films on whitewater kayaking. One of these is the internationally acclaimed "Sick Line" series.

Nouria Newman, 15, on her way to fourth place in the women's class at the 2007 French Slalom Championships

Whitewater is full of young talent. They are setting new standards and pushing the sport forward.

French kayaker Nouria Newman started paddling with a local kayak club when she was 5 years old. Now she excels in many different types of kayaking and has been a member of both the French slalom and freestyle teams. At the age of 15, she came in third at the World Freestyle Championships and placed fourth overall in the women's class at the French Slalom Championships.

Dane Jackson masters the Bus Eater wave of the Ottawa River in Canada.

Emily Jackson has already claimed the title of junior women's World Freestyle Champion. Not to be outdone by his sister, Dane came in third in the World Freestyle Championships when he was only 14 years old. He has won dozens of competitions all over the United States — he's even beaten his dad! Emily and Dane have both paddled on the Zambezi and Nile rivers in Africa. They also actively support charity work in Africa by donating some of their competition winnings to help educate Ugandan children.

Emily Jackson demonstrates a Mega-Back Blunt.

With Eric Jackson as their father, it is hardly surprising that Emily and Dane Jackson are two of the best junior kayakers in the world. They spend six months each year touring the United States. They travel from river to river and take part in competitions. Their mom makes sure they keep up with their schoolwork!

No matter how sophisticated the equipment, kayaking will always remain a high-risk sport. This is the real-life story of three experienced kayakers who were exposed to the dangers of whitewater with near-fatal consequences.

In the spring of 1999, U.S. kayaker Joey Kentucky and U.K. kayakers Andy Round and Simon Westgarth decided to take a trip on the Little White Salmon River in Oregon. A popular river with whitewater kayakers, the Little White Salmon includes a 33-foot (10-m) waterfall – the Spirit Falls.

The three paddlers reached Spirit Falls after an eventful day. Joey paddled over the waterfall first, landing well, it seemed. But suddenly he was pushed to the left, with the water knocking him over.

Every time Joey recovered, the water knocked him over again. He continued to fight the water until, out of breath and exhausted, he exited his kayak and began to float unconscious down the river.

Andy and Simon chased Joey down the river. As soon as they got ahold of him, Simon gave him emergency resuscitation. Joey began to gasp for air. Within five minutes he'd regained consciousness. Now they had to get out. They had three options – paddle out, climb out, or stay put. They decided to climb out, all the time keeping Joey warm and moving closer to getting help.

Once back at their vehicle, they sped Joey to a hospital. Doctors found that his heart had too much lactic acid and was beating out of rhythm. Lactic acid is formed in the body's muscles during very heavy exercise, when the need for oxygen exceeds the amount that the body can provide. It stiffens the muscles and causes them to ache. In this case, it had been Joey's heart – one of the most important muscles in the body, of course – that had been producing the lactic acid. The acid had stiffened Joey's heart and almost stopped it from beating.

Luckily, the slow climb helped Joey's body transport oxygen to his heart and gradually remove the lactic acid. So it was thanks to Joey's team that he lived to tell the story!

Simon (left) and Joey (right) take a break between rapids, a few days after Joey's accident. Joey was lucky enough to have a full recovery.

1869 – John Wesley Powell, with nine men, four boats, and food, explores the Grand Canyon in Colorado for ten months.

1936 – Canoeing and kayaking on flatwater become Olympic sports at the Berlin Olympic Games.

1960 – Boats made of fiberglass, which is light and extremely tough, allow kayakers to paddle over many obstacles. Previously, they had needed to get out of the water to carry their kayaks around.

1969 – Mike Jones, Jeff Slater, Dave Allen, and two others paddle the upper sections of Switzerland's River Inn, known as the hardest stretch of water in Europe. Jones was 17 at the time.

1971 – Walt Blackader tackles the Turnback Canyon on the Alsek River in Canada and Alaska. It is of North America's most difficult stretches of water. On completion, he says he was lucky to have survived.

1971 – The first Himalayan kayak expedition, on the Kali Gandaki River, is led by Hans Memminger. Until then, this stretch of river had been considered impossible to tackle.

1972 – Whitewater slalom takes place at the Munich Olympic Games, with racing on the city of Augsburg's specially constructed Eiskanal. It is the first artificial whitewater course of its kind.

1972 – Mike Jones, Mick Hopkinson, Dave Burkinshaw, Glen Greer, and Steve Nash complete the first descent of more than 200 miles (320 km) of the Blue Nile River in Ethiopia.

Highest river

The source of Mount Everest's Dudh Kosi River is the Khumbu Glacier, some 17,500 feet (6,000 m) above sea level. In 1976, a team of British kayakers, led by Mike Jones, tackle the river's treacherous whitewater.

1978 – Lars Holbeck and Chuck Stanley begin their ten years of serious Grade 5 kayaking in the Sierra Nevada mountain range in California.

1980 – Kayaks are made from plastics instead of fiberglass.

1987 – The dry paddling jacket is developed. It is made with waterproof fabric.

1990 – Mick Hopkinson makes the first descent of the gigantic Grade 5 Nevis Bluff rapid on the Kawara River in New Zealand.

2002 – Scott Lindgren, Mike Abbott, Alan Ellard, Johnnie and Willie Kern, Dustin Knapp, and Steve Fisher paddle the Tsangpo Gorge in Tibet.

2004 – A team of paddlers complete the Seven Rivers Expedition by paddling seven major multi-day trips all on Grade 5 water in California for fifty straight days. Rivers traveled include the famous Upper Cherry Creek and San Joaquin.

2004 – The Source to Sea Expedition ends successfully when an international team of kayakers reaches the Mediterranean Sea. They had spent the previous four and a half months paddling the length of the White Nile and Nile rivers in Africa.

2005 – The first one-day descent of Canada's Grand Canyon of the 60-mile (100-km) Stikine River is made by U.S. paddlers Tommy Hilleke, Toby McDermott, Daniel DeLavergne, and John Grace. Previous trips had taken three days.

2007 – German kayaker Felix Lämmler sets a new world record for free fall kayaking down a waterfall. He descends a dramatic 111.5 feet (34 m) down the Leuenfall Waterfall in Switzerland.

All in a day

In 2005, the Upper Cherry Creek in California is completed by American paddlers in just one day. They finish an arduous 11-mile (17.75-km) hike in five hours, setting off at three o'clock in the morning. This is then followed by six and a half hours of paddling on Grade 5 rapids. Previous attempts had taken one day to hike in and two days to paddle out.

Glossary

Blade The wide piece at the end of a paddle used to push against the water

Boil A pressurized section of water, often where two currents meet

Bow The front of a boat

Broach To become caught against an obstruction and turned sideways by the current. A very dangerous situation.

Canoe A light, narrow, open boat propelled by one or more paddlers in a kneeling position. Canoeists use single-bladed paddles, alternating strokes from one side of the canoe to the other. Canoes are not generally used on whitewater.

Canyon A rock gorge with extremely steep sides

Carbon fiber A synthetic, lightweight material made from woven carbon thread

Cartwheel A freestyle move where the kayak rotates vertically end over end

Class Another name for Grade

Cockpit The space in a kayak where the paddler sits

Creeking A type of kayaking that involves descending very steep, low-volume whitewater. It is much more dangerous and extreme than other types of kayaking.

Deck The covered area over the top of a boat that keeps water out

Downstream The direction in which the river is flowing

Extreme racing Paddling a kayak down a section of hard whitewater requiring excellent boat-handling skills. The rivers are typically Grade 5 and involve waterfalls and dangerous rapids.

Fiberglass A tough, synthetic, lightweight material made from glass fibers.

Flatwater Calm water, found on a slow-moving river or a lake.

Freestyle Where a paddler performs tricks, usually in a static river wave or a hole

Gate Two striped poles suspended just above the water on a slalom course

Gorge A deep, narrow, rocky valley with a river

Grade The classification given to a piece of water to show how difficult and dangerous it is. Also called Class.

Hole Where water goes over a rock that forces it back on itself

Hull The underside of the boat

Kayak Any of the various boat designs imitating the Inuit hunting kayak with a watertight enclosed top. Kayakers use a paddle with a blade at each end of the shaft.

Life jacket A buoyant jacket designed to keep paddlers on the surface of the water if they fall in. Also called a PFD.

Line The route paddlers choose to take through a rapid

Mystery Move A freestyle move where a paddler uses the river's currents to submerge the boat underneath the water's surface

Paddler A kayaker or canoeist

PFD Personal flotation device. Also called a life jacket.

River left The left side of a river when going downstream

River right The right side of a river when going downstream

Shaft The long part of a paddle gripped by the paddler

Slalom A contest in which paddlers negotiate a series of gates

Slide Water flowing over an area of smooth bedrock

Spray skirt A piece of gear used to seal the area between a paddler's waist and the boat's cockpit, making it watertight

Stern The back of a boat

Sumerian Ancient civilization in what is now southeast Iraq

Upstream Opposite to the direction the river is flowing

Whitewater Turbulent water that is full of air, resulting from water flowing around and over obstacles in its path

Index

About the Author

Deb Pinniger is one of the world's leading female expedition paddlers, and has been kayaking for more than twenty years. She has competed in contests throughout the world, winning the World Freestyle Championship twice. Deb also works as a kayak teacher, and has led groups of children on kayak exhibitions from Africa to Europe. Her writing has been published in many outdoor magazines, newspapers, and books.